Deepfake Defense 2025

AI-Driven Strategies for Synthetic Media Detection

Taylor Royce

DEDICATION

To the unwavering truth-seekers, the guardians of digital integrity, and the trailblazers paving the way for a time when genuineness will rule the day.

To the scientists, programmers, and moral AI trailblazers who put forth endless effort to expose fraud and preserve confidence in a world of artificial intelligence.

To the journalists, educators, and legislators who work to preserve, inform, and promote the principles of accountability and openness.

And to those who are unwilling to be duped may your inquisitiveness, alertness, and discernment keep illuminating the way to a more secure and honest digital environment.

DISCLAIMER

This book is meant solely for educational and informational purposes. Although every attempt has been taken to guarantee the quality and dependability of the material provided, neither the author nor the publisher expressly nor implicitly offer any guarantees or assurances about the content's completeness, accuracy, or applicability.

At the time of publication, the topic on deepfakes, synthetic media, AI technologies, and cybersecurity precautions was grounded in the most recent findings and research. Nonetheless, given how quickly digital forensics and artificial intelligence are developing, additional advancements might appear that are not discussed in this book. For the most recent information, readers are urged to speak with legal experts, cybersecurity specialists, and other sources.

There is no technical, financial, or legal advice in this book. The publisher and author disclaim all responsibility for any direct or indirect effects that may result from the use or abuse of the information presented here. Any mentions of particular businesses, organizations, or technologies are merely meant to serve as examples and do not imply affiliations or endorsements.

You understand that you alone are in charge of how you understand and use the material in this book

CONTENTS

ACKNOWLEDGMENTS

Writing this book has involved much research, education, and in-depth contemplation of the rapidly changing fields of digital security and artificial intelligence. Without the assistance, insights, and contributions of several people and organizations, this effort would not have been feasible.

First and first, I want to express my sincere gratitude to the scientists, researchers, and professionals in the fields of artificial intelligence, cybersecurity, and digital forensics whose innovative work has helped us better comprehend deepfakes and synthetic media. Their commitment to developing technology while ensuring its moral application has been admirable.

I would also like to thank my peers, mentors, and coworkers for their insightful comments, insightful conversations, and critical viewpoints that enhanced the caliber and depth of this book. Your knowledge and perceptions have been crucial in forming the material and guaranteeing its applicability in the current digital environment.

For their constant encouragement, tolerance, and support during this writing process, I am also incredibly appreciative of my friends and family. Your confidence in this endeavor has consistently served as a source of inspiration.

Finally, this book is for readers who want to comprehend, fight, and negotiate the complicated world of AI-generated media. I hope it will educate you, motivate you to take action, and help create a more safe and knowledgeable digital future.

Many thanks to all of you.

CHAPTER 1

THE EMERGENCE OF DEEPFAKES AND SYNTHETIC MEDIA

1.1 Comprehending Synthetic Media: Meanings and Categories of Artificial Intelligence-Generated Content

User: Let's start with the fundamentals of AI. What is synthetic media, exactly?

AI: Yes! Content produced or modified by artificial intelligence, including text, audio, video, and image, is referred to as synthetic media. Synthetic media uses cutting-edge machine learning techniques, such as Generative Adversarial Networks (GANs) and diffusion models, to create incredibly realistic yet fake content, in contrast to traditional media, which depends on human input at every stage.

User: That sounds too general. Are synthetic media and deepfakes the same thing?

AI: One type of synthetic media is deepfakes. The field encompasses a wide range of AI-generated content, including:

AI-generated movies that modify a person's face, voice, or complete body to produce incredibly convincing yet phony footage are known as "Deepfake Videos."

- **AI-Generated Images:** From text prompts, tools such as DALL·E and Stable Diffusion produce realistic or creative images.
- **Synthetic Speech:** AI-driven voice cloning technology can remarkably accurately replicate human voices.
- **AI-Written Text:** Text that imitates human writing styles is produced using large language models (LLMs), such as GPT-4.
- **AI Avatars & Virtual Influencers**: AI-generated characters, such as Lil Miquela, are fully digital but behave like actual social media influencers.

User: Synthetic media isn't necessarily harmful, isn't it?

AI: Indeed! There are valid uses for synthetic media in marketing, accessibility, education, and entertainment. But the same technology can also be abused, which can result in fraud, false information, and moral quandaries.

1.2 Deepfake Development: From Face Swaps to Extremely Lifelike Video Editing

User: What was the evolution of deepfakes? The deepfakes of today look far more sophisticated than the face-swapping applications of the past, which I remember.

AI: You are entirely correct. Over time, deepfake technology has advanced quickly thanks to open-source software, improved processing power, and AI developments. Let's examine its development in detail:

1. In the early 2010s, machine learning models that could create faces from datasets were first experimented with by academic researchers. This marked the beginning of AI-generated faces.

- Due to their limitations, these models frequently produced skewed or fuzzy outputs.

2. In 2014, Ian Goodfellow and his colleagues unveiled GANs (Generative Adversarial Networks), a revolutionary technology that allowed artificial intelligence to produce incredibly lifelike visuals.

- The generator and discriminator neural networks that make up GANs compete to make the generated images more realistic.

3. 2017 – The Rise of Deepfake Videos: The first identifiable deepfake movies were created when hobbyists started swapping faces in videos using autoencoders. These deepfakes were initially of terrible quality, with obvious hiccups and awkward lip-syncing.

4. 2019-Hyper-Realistic Deepfake Boom: AI models grew increasingly potent, creating incredibly lifelike deepfake videos.

- Concerns over the possible abuse of deepfakes in political disinformation and cybercrime were first voiced by researchers and tech firms.

5. 2022–2024 – Real-Time Deepfake Manipulation: AI

developments made it possible to create deepfakes in real time, in which a person's voice and face may be altered during live broadcasts or video chats. This was disturbing as well as amazing because it became harder to tell the difference between authentic and fraudulent video.

6. 2025 - Creation Arms Race vs. Deepfake Detection: As new algorithms are developed to fight each new manipulation technique, deepfake production and detection technologies are engaged in a never-ending battle.

User: What a dramatic progression! Is it still simple to identify deepfakes?

AI: Regretfully, no. Deepfakes nowadays are nearly identical to authentic content. Particularly in the areas of politics, cybersecurity, and digital trust, this has significant ramifications.

1.3 Deepfakes' Social and Ethical Consequences

User: Why are deepfakes so harmful?

AI: Because deepfakes erode confidence in digital content, they pose serious hazards. The following are some of the main issues:

Fake News & Misinformation:

Videos produced by AI have the ability to make false political claims, which can cause anxiety and uncertainty.

- For instance, a deepfake video purporting to show a world leader announcing war may trigger widespread panic.

Cybercrime & Financial Fraud: Deepfake audio can be used to authorize fraudulent transactions and pose as executives.

- Example: When crooks instructed an employee to transfer money using an AI-cloned CEO voice, a company lost millions.

Privacy Violations & Non-Consensual Deepfake Content: Deepfake pornography is becoming more and more of a problem, frequently aimed at private individuals and celebrities.

- For instance, victims may suffer psychological and

reputational injury when their faces are unconsentedly featured on obscene videos.

Erosion of Trust in Journalism & Media: The legitimacy of media outlets is in jeopardy if people are unable to discriminate between authentic and fraudulent news.

- For instance, fabricated interviews or manipulated news stories have the potential to sway public opinion on important topics.

User: So reality could be totally distorted by deepfakes?

AI: Indeed! It is more difficult to believe video evidence when deepfakes are convincing, which makes it simpler for malicious actors to disseminate false information or dismiss actual events as "fake news."

1.4 Legal and Regulatory Obstacles in the Battle Against Synthetic Media

User: Are deepfakes governed by any laws?

AI: The legal environment is constantly changing, but

some countries have begun enforcing rules. Below is a summary of ongoing initiatives:

Watermarking AI-generated content is required by the DEEPFAKES Accountability Act (proposed) in the United States.

- Malicious deepfakes pertaining to elections and revenge pornography are prohibited in California.

According to the AI Act, deepfake technology is a high-risk application that needs to be regulated in the European Union.

China: To avoid disinformation, the Deep Synthesis Regulation requires that content produced by AI be tagged.

User: That's a beginning, but do these laws work?

AI: Enforcement is still challenging because:

- **Anonymity of Deepfake Creators:** A large number of them work outside of legal jurisdictions.
- **Quick AI Developments:** Laws are unable to keep up with the rapidly changing technology.

- **Difficulties in Proving Damage:** Legal action necessitates proof of impact and intent, which is difficult to provide in deepfake cases.

User: What is the answer, then?

AI: A multifaceted strategy is required:

- **AI-Powered Detection Tools:** Organizations such as Google and Microsoft are creating AI models to detect deepfakes.
- **Authentication of Content Based on Blockchain:** Blockchain technology can offer unchangeable evidence of original content.
- **Education & Public Awareness:** Digital literacy initiatives can assist individuals in identifying deepfakes.

User: It seems like an endless struggle.

AI: Yes, it is! In order to maintain digital trust and security, governments, tech businesses, and the general public must work together to combat deepfakes, which is a continuous problem.

CHAPTER 2

ATTACKERS VS. DEFENDERS IN THE AI ARMS RACE

Rapidly developing artificial intelligence is driving an arms race between those who create deepfakes and those who attempt to identify them. The defensive techniques used to detect and combat generative models must advance along with them. This chapter explores the core technology underlying the creation of deepfakes, the changing strategies of adversarial AI, and the state-of-the-art instruments for identifying and thwarting synthetic media.

2.1 The Diffusion Models, Transformers, and GANs That Underlie Deepfakes

Strong AI models that allow for the production of incredibly lifelike synthetic media are at the heart of deepfake generation. Generative Adversarial Networks (GANs), Transformers, and Diffusion Models are the three most important architectures in this field. Deepfakes are becoming more and more realistic due to the distinct characteristics of each of these technologies.

GANs (Generative Adversarial Networks)

GANs introduced a dual-network technique that transformed the production of deepfakes:

- The generator creates artificial images, movies, or audio that are hard to tell apart from actual data.
- **The Discriminator:** Assesses the created content's legitimacy and gives the generator input to enhance its results.

Because of this adversarial connection, GANs are able to iteratively improve their output, producing deepfakes that can remarkably accurately replicate real-world data.

Transformers and Mechanisms of Self-Attention

Deepfake generation has made use of transformers, which were first created for natural language processing. Their capacity to examine linkages and context in vast datasets makes them especially helpful for: AI-generated speech synthesis, in which voice models pick up accent and intonation.

- **AI-driven face reenactment** involves altering the movements and facial expressions in recordings
- AI can now create realistic scenarios from textual descriptions thanks to text-to-video generation.

The coherence of created material is improved by Transformers' self-attention mechanism, which allows them to take into account many factors at once.

The Next Frontier: Diffusion Models

A significant advancement in AI-generated images and video synthesis is represented by diffusion models. Diffusion models function differently than GANs, which employ an adversarial approach, by:

1. Making random noise first.
2. Creating a realistic image or video by gradually improving the noise across several iterations.

Because of this process, diffusion models are incredibly good at producing detailed, high-resolution information with less artifacts than GANs, which results in more realistic deepfakes.

2.2 Adversarial AI: The Development of Methods for Producing Deepfakes

Attackers have been improving their methods to circumvent detection systems as AI-generated media has advanced. Among the most notable developments in the production of deepfakes are:

One-Shot and Few-Shot Learning

1. To get realistic results, traditional deepfake models needed substantial datasets of a person's voice or face.

- Modern AI can produce deepfakes with little input by applying few-shot or one-shot learning, often with just a single image or a brief audio clip. This significantly reduces the obstacle for malevolent actors, allowing for the quick creation of convincing fakes.

2. StyleGAN and Hyper-Realistic Face Synthesis
StyleGAN innovations enable deepfakes to be produced with microexpressions, lighting, and skin texture, among other finer features, making them extremely hard to tell

apart from authentic footage.

- Artificial intelligence (AI) models can now produce synthetic humans, which are faces that look entirely realistic but do not belong to any real person.

3. AI-Enhanced Face Reenactment and Lip-Syncing

Deepfake technology has advanced to synchronize lip movements with generated speech, making it exceedingly difficult to identify mismatched dubbing.

- The distinction between real and fake media is further blurred by face reenactment models, such as DeepFaceLab and First Order Motion Model, which let users alter facial expressions in real time.

4. Cross-Modal Deepfakes (Voice and Video)

Some deepfake tools can now create whole multimedia forgeries by using a text input to create both voice and face movements.

- These multimodal models are especially risky for cyber crime, political disinformation, and impersonation schemes.

The threat posed by deepfake technology increases with its

accessibility, requiring increasingly complex detection techniques.

2.3 AI-Powered Detection and Authentication Systems to Combat Deepfakes

AI-driven detection methods have advanced as a result of the deepfake generation's quick evolution. The following are the best methods for spotting fake media:

1. Forensic Analysis Driven by AI

Deep learning is used by detection models to find small inconsistencies in skin texture, eye reflections, and facial features.

- To ascertain authenticity, sophisticated classifiers examine biometric signals, such as the detection of pulses in video material.

2. Analysis of Frequency Domain

The frequency spectrum is the sole way to identify artifacts unseen to the human eye that are frequently present in deepfake videos.

- These irregularities can be detected by AI models

trained on Fourier transforms, indicating possible forgeries.

In order to timestamp and validate original media and make sure that any changes can be identified, emerging solutions employ blockchain technology for

3. Blockchain-Based Content Authentication.

Cryptographic signatures are applied to content at the time of capture by platforms such as Truepic and Amber Authenticate.

The absence of appropriate metadata AI-generated material makes it simpler to detect and flag corrupted content. This is why watermarking and metadata verification are important.

Pixel-level digital watermarks can assist in authenticating authentic media and guard against unwanted alteration.

Real-time monitoring and verification are essential since deepfake producers are constantly improving their techniques to evade detection in spite of these countermeasures.

2.4 Post-processing vs. Real-Time Detection: Advantages and Disadvantages

Real-time analysis and post-processing forensic examination are the two main methods for detecting deepfakes. Each has unique benefits and drawbacks.

1. Real-Time Detection

- AI-driven technologies examine media as it is uploaded or broadcast in order to identify irregularities.
- To stop false information from propagating, social media sites and streaming services use deepfake detection filters.
- One of its strengths is its ability to intervene quickly and stop the spread of altered content.
- Its high computing cost and susceptibility to evasion tactics (such as introducing noise to evade detection) are its weaknesses.

Media after it has been recorded or shared is analyzed by deepfake detection algorithms.

2. Post-Processing Forensic Analysis.

- Methods include metadata inspection, reverse image searches, and frame-by-frame analysis.

- Because processing time is not a constraint, the accuracy is higher.

- **Weaknesses:** A delayed response could result in harm from false information already done.

In order to successfully combat deepfakes, both strategies must be applied simultaneously. While post-processing techniques provide deeper forensic analysis for long-term digital security, real-time monitoring helps avert urgent threats.

Cutting-edge developments in machine learning are fueling the continuing AI arms race between deepfake producers and defenders. Defenders are creating AI-powered detection tools, cryptographic authentication systems, and forensic analysis techniques to combat attackers that use GANs, transformers, and diffusion models to create nearly flawless forgeries.

The integrity of digital media will depend on cooperation

between AI researchers, cybersecurity professionals, and policymakers as deepfake technology develops further. The reliability of internet content and the capacity to separate fact from fiction in a world growing more and more artificial will be determined by the outcome of this arms race.

CHAPTER 3

NEXT-GEN ALGORITHMS' FUNCTION IN DEEPFAKE IDENTIFICATION

Traditional detection techniques are finding it difficult to keep up with the increasing sophistication of deepfake technology. The next step in deepfake detection is represented by the transition from convolutional neural networks (CNNs) to transformer-based models, the incorporation of explainable AI, and the emergence of few-shot learning and federated learning. These developments seek to retain strong protection against manipulated media while improving accuracy, transparency, and user privacy.

3.1 Transformer-Based Detection Models for Improved Accuracy: Going Beyond CNNs

Convolutional neural networks (CNNs) dominated image and video analysis for many years. CNNs are susceptible to developing deepfake techniques because, although they are excellent at identifying patterns and extracting features, they have trouble with high-dimensional data and long-range relationships.

Restrictions of CNN-Based Deepfake Detection

- **Local Feature Dependence:** CNNs are vulnerable to complex deepfake artifacts that cover wider areas because they mainly examine small portions of an image.

- **Lack of Context Awareness:** They have trouble recognizing global relationships in a sequence of images or videos.

- **Adversarial Attack Vulnerability:** To fool CNN-based detectors, attackers can covertly alter pixel-level features.

How Transformer-Based Models Enhance the Identification of Deepfakes

Deepfake detection has been transformed by transformers, especially vision transformers (ViTs), which introduce self-attention mechanisms that enable models to examine complete images holistically. Among the main benefits are:

- **Global Context Awareness** Transformers assess relationships over a complete image, making them more resistant to manipulation than CNNs, which concentrate on local patches.

- **More Precision in Time Analysis:** Changes take place across several frames in video deepfakes. Transformers that assess temporal and spatial dependencies, such as **TimeSformer**, improve the accuracy of detection.

- Transformers are more adept at spotting discrepancies across several levels of abstraction, which makes it more difficult for attackers to evade detection. This makes them resilient to adversarial attacks.

According to recent studies, hybrid models combining CNNs and transformers produce even better outcomes by utilizing the contextual awareness of transformers and the feature extraction power of CNNs. The move to transformer-based models will be essential to staying ahead of attackers as deepfake threats change.

3.2 Deepfake Detection with Explainable AI (XAI): Openness in Decision Making

The black-box nature Deep learning models are one of the main obstacles to AI-driven deepfake detection. Users frequently don't know why a piece of material was flagged as a deepfake by a detection algorithm. Explainable AI (XAI) can help with this.

Why XAI is Essential in Deepfake Detection

- **Building Trust in AI Systems:** Users are more inclined to believe a model's predictions if they comprehend how it comes to them.
- In order to identify and rectify biases in deepfake detection algorithms, researchers can use XAI.
- **Compliance with Regulations:** To support content filtering choices in legal and journalistic contexts, transparency is crucial.

The Use of XAI in Deepfake Detection

- **Feature Attribution Methods:** Methods such as Grad-CAM (Gradient-weighted Class Activation

Mapping) show which parts of a picture made the biggest contribution to the deepfake classification.

- **Saliency Maps:** These show regions where the AI model identified irregularities, such irregular lighting or unusual eye movement.

- **Decision Trees and Rule-Based Explanations:** AI models are able to produce explanations for their classifications that are understandable by humans, giving a clear picture of the reasons for a media item's flagging.

For instance, a XAI-enabled system could provide the following explanation if a detection model finds a deepfake video of a politician:

- "Detected inconsistency in facial expressions between frames."
- "Unnatural blinking pattern observed."
- "Lack of microexpressions typical of real human speech."

Organizations may improve accountability, boost model performance, and win public trust in AI-driven content authentication by incorporating XAI into deepfake detection pipelines.

3.3 Identifying Hidden Deepfake Variations with Few-Shot and Zero-Shot Learning

The continual emergence of new deepfake approaches is one of the biggest hurdles in deepfake detection. Previously undiscovered manipulation techniques may go undetected by a model trained on prior deepfake. Herein lies the role of few-shot and zero-shot learning.

Minimum Data Training with Few-Shot Learning

AI models can identify deepfakes with very minimal training data thanks to few-shot learning.

These models learn to generalize from just a handful of examples rather than millions of instances.

- For identifying newly constructed deepfake algorithms that haven't been thoroughly documented, this is really helpful.

Detection of Deepfakes Without Previous Training: Zero-Shot Learning

This is further enhanced by zero-shot learning, which

enables a model to identify deepfakes it has never encountered using learnt representations of authenticity.

An AI model, for example, can identify abnormalities in deepfakes even if it has never seen that particular manipulation technique before if it is aware of biometric indicators of genuine human faces.

Real-World Uses of Few-Shot and Zero-Shot Learning

- **Cybersecurity & Law Enforcement:** Identifying recently developed identity fraud efforts and deepfake frauds.

- **Journalism & Fact-Checking:** Real-time detection of false information produced by deepfakes.

- Adjusting to changing deepfake trends without requiring a lot of retraining is possible using Social Media Content Moderation.

few-shot and zero-shot learning will be crucial for sustaining proactive and adaptive detection systems as deepfake techniques advance in complexity.

3.4 Privacy-Preserving AI Training via Federated Learning for Deepfake Detection

Data privacy is a key issue in deepfake detection. Large volumes of training data are needed for traditional AI models, and these data are frequently taken from sensitive or personal user content. Federated learning enables AI models to be trained without centralizing user data, providing a privacy-preserving alternative.

How Federated Learning Works

- Federated learning trains AI models locally on user devices as opposed to uploading raw data to a central server.
- Every gadget advances the model without disclosing private information to outside servers.
- Only model updates (not raw data) are supplied to a central server for aggregation following training.

Enhanced Privacy: Private video and biometric information never leaves the user's device. This is one of the advantages of federated learning for deepfake detection.

Scalability: Without the need for centralized storage, millions of devices can help refine the model.

- Federated models have the capacity to continually learn from novel deepfake patterns without disclosing user information.

Federated Learning Use Cases in Deepfake Detection

- **Mobile Security Apps:** Federated learning makes it possible to detect deepfakes using smartphones without jeopardizing user privacy.

- **Corporate AI Systems**: Businesses can use federated deepfake detection without exchanging confidential information.

- **Decentralized Social Media Moderation:** Without centralized monitoring, platforms can report deepfake content in a dispersed fashion.

AI-driven deepfake detection may balance accuracy, scalability, and user privacy by incorporating federated learning, guaranteeing strong defense against synthetic media without sacrificing morality.

Cutting-edge AI developments are necessary to combat

deepfakes. Although CNNs have traditionally dominated image analysis, transformer-based models have emerged as a better alternative with improved contextual awareness and accuracy. In the meantime, deepfake detection is transparent thanks to Explainable AI (XAI), which contributes to the development of confidence in AI-driven moderation.

Few-shot and zero-shot learning make detection systems more resilient by allowing models to adapt to new deepfake approaches with minimal or no prior training. Lastly, federated learning provides a privacy-first strategy that lets AI models advance without jeopardizing user data.

These next-generation AI strategies will be vital in protecting truth and authenticity in the digital world as deepfake technology continues to advance.

CHAPTER 4

DEEPFAKES BASED ON TEXT AND AUDIO: AN INCREASING DANGER

Although deepfake technology first became well-known for producing incredibly lifelike spoof films, as artificial intelligence has advanced, it has now also been used to create audio and text-based deepfakes. Currently, fraud, misinformation, political propaganda, and cybercrimes are being committed using these AI-generated manipulations. Differentiating between actual and synthetic information is getting harder as machine learning, natural language processing (NLP), and text-to-speech (TTS) models progress.

The mechanisms of AI-synthesized voices, audio deepfake detection methods, the function of natural language processing in text-based disinformation, and methods for developing strong multimodal detection systems are all covered in this chapter.

4.1 Artificial Intelligence-Generated Voices: How Text-to-Speech (TTS) Models Recreate Natural Voices

From monotonous, robotic voices to near-perfect voice clones that can mimic tone, pitch, and even subtle emotional cues, text-to-speech (TTS) technology has advanced significantly. With the ability to produce speech that is identical to human speech, AI-powered voice synthesis has become a powerful tool but also a dangerous weapon.

How Voices Synthesized by AI Operate

Deep learning models that have been trained on hours of actual human speech are used in contemporary voice cloning techniques. These models are able to produce artificial speech that records:

Pronunciation and Accent

- Copying local accents and linguistic quirks.
- Emotional Tone: Changing the voice output to sound neutral, angry, sad, or joyful.
- Replicating a particular person's vocal signature is

known as Speaker Identity.

In AI voice synthesis, the two most popular designs are:

The first is WaveNet (by DeepMind), a deep generative model that generates incredibly lifelike speech waveforms.

- makes predictions and synthesizes audio samples using a probabilistic method.

The second model is called Tacotron + Vocoder Models

- **Tacotron 2,** which was created by Google, transforms text into a spectrogram.
- The spectrogram is subsequently transformed into an audio waveform with a vocoder like as WaveGlow or Parallel WaveGAN.

Very minimal training data is needed for these models. AI is a perfect weapon for social engineering assaults, impersonation fraud, and political disinformation since it can create a very realistic voice replica from just a few minutes of recorded speech.

4.2 Identifying Audio Deepfakes: Machine Learning and Spectral Analysis Methods

Traditional detection methods based on human judgment are losing their effectiveness as AI-generated voices become more lifelike. Automated detection is crucial since a trained machine learning model can frequently deceive even experts.

Main Features of AI-Synthesized Voices

- **Lack of Natural Breath Sounds**: Human speech's subtle inhalations and exhalations are frequently not replicated by AI-generated voices.
- Rhythmic Inconsistencies Deepfake voices can occasionally display unusual uniformity in pacing, in contrast to the natural variation of real speech.
- **Spectral Artifacts:** AI-generated voices may have frequency artifacts or unnatural digital noise that is different from natural human speech.

Advanced Detection Techniques
1. Spectral and Acoustic Analysis
- To identify irregularities, machine learning models

can examine frequency spectrograms of authentic versus fraudulent speech.

- Voices produced by AI frequently lack high-frequency variations that are found in natural speech.

2. Deep Neural Networks & Machine Learning

- **Convolutional Neural Networks (CNNs)** are able to identify whether audio is authentic or not by using acoustic qualities that they have learned.
- Over time, speech is analyzed using Recurrent Neural Networks (RNNs), which identify minute anomalies in voice synthesis.

3. AI-Driven Phoneme Analysis

- The smallest units of spoken sound are called phonemes.
- Rare phonemes are frequently mispronounced or blended unnaturally by AI-generated voices.
- Phoneme patterns can be compared to the known speech patterns of a real speaker via a detection model.

The use of AI-powered forensic tools by law enforcement agencies to compare deepfake voices to genuine recordings and identify manipulation is known as Forensic Voice Profiling.

Preventing voice-based fraud, impersonation schemes, and deepfake-generated misinformation campaigns requires the use of these detection techniques.

4.3 Misinformation and Textual Deepfakes: NLP-Based Deceit in Fake News

A developing concern in addition to audio deepfakes are text-based deepfakes, which are fueled by advanced Natural Language Processing (NLP) models such as GPT-4 and others. These AI models have the ability to create incredibly realistic fake news pieces, write impersonations of people, and influence public opinion at large scales.

The Mechanism of NLP-Based Deepfakes

Large-scale human language datasets are used to train AI text creation algorithms, which allow them to:

AI is capable of producing text that mimics a person's tone and phrasing through the use of Mimic Writing Styles.

- Constructing fictitious stories that seem to originate from reliable sources is known as "fabricating fake news."
- Automate Social Media Manipulation: Using bot networks to quickly disseminate false content.

Typical Types of Text-Based Deepfakes

- **Fake News Articles:** artificial intelligence-generated news items intended to disseminate misleading information.
- Phishing emails are extremely customized emails that imitate authentic communication methods.
- Deepfake Social Media Posts: Artificial intelligence-generated content posted by phony accounts to influence conversations.

The use of phony customer reviews to enhance or damage business reputations is known as "synthetic product reviews."

Identifying Text-Based Deepfakes

NLP-based detection tools examine the following in order to counteract AI-generated disinformation:

- **Perplexity Scores:** AI-generated content is more structured than human writing and typically has less unpredictability.
- **Semantic Inconsistencies:** AI is capable of producing grammatically sound but illogical phrases.
- **Metadata Analysis:** Finding anomalies in digital footprints and odd posting behaviors.
- **Linguistic Fingerprinting:** Identifies impersonation attempts by comparing AI-generated text to recognized writing samples.

A mix of automated detection technologies, media literacy instruction, and strong fact-checking mechanisms is needed to combat AI-generated disinformation.

4.4 Developing Sturdy Detection Systems for Deepfake Multimodal Threats

The rise of deepfake technology in text, audio, and video formats necessitates the use of multimodal detection systems to counter these threats.

Difficulties in Multimodal Deepfake Detection

- **Cross-Domain Attacks:** To produce more convincing manipulations, attackers frequently combine fake text, fake audio, and false video.

- Rapid Evolution of AI Models: To combat emerging deepfake approaches, detection systems need to be updated on a regular basis.

- Social media companies and governmental organizations require systems that can identify deepfakes at scale without incurring significant computing expenses.

Developing a Framework for Multimodal Detection

A strong detection system ought to incorporate:

1. Audio-Visual Synchronization Checks: Deepfake videos frequently feature speech patterns and lip movements that are not in sync.

- Artificial intelligence algorithms are able to identify discrepancies by comparing facial movements to speech rhythm.

2. The accuracy of detection can be increased by combining the analysis of voiceprints, writing styles, and video artifacts in Cross-Modal Anomaly Detection.

3. Using blockchain technology to confirm the validity of media content before its dissemination is known as Blockchain for Content Authentication.

Reducing false positives by combining automated AI detection with human fact-checkers is the fourth step in the Human-AI Collaboration process.

In a time when it's getting more difficult to tell the difference between synthetic and real media, we may create strong defenses against AI-generated deception by combining these strategies.

Deepfakes based on text and audio pose an increasing threat to cybersecurity and disinformation. Social engineering and fraud are made possible by the ability of AI-generated voices to mimic real people. Disinformation campaigns are fueled by textual deepfakes, which distort public opinion and harm reputations.

Advanced detection techniques such as spectrum analysis, NLP-based text detection, and multimodal AI systems are essential in order to counter these threats. In order to protect digital authenticity, deepfake detection will require constant innovation, cooperation between AI researchers and cybersecurity specialists, and proactive regulatory measures.

CHAPTER 5

DATASET DIFFICULTIES AND PREJUDICE IN DEEPFAKE IDENTIFICATION

The strength of deepfake detection depends on the quality of the training data. Deepfake detection methods run the risk of being ineffective or, worse, biased against particular populations in the absence of diverse, representative, and high-quality datasets. This chapter explores the ethical issues surrounding the use of open versus proprietary datasets, the difficulties in curating datasets for deepfake detection, and the function of data augmentation in enhancing model resilience.

5.1 Managing Superior Deepfake Datasets: Diversity and Representativeness Concerns

Any deepfake detection system must be trained on a high-quality, diverse, and well-labeled dataset in order to function properly. Curating such a dataset, however, comes with a number of difficulties, such as:

Issues with Data Scarcity and Quality

1. Lack of Realistic Deepfake Samples: The majority of datasets are less reflective of the most recent AI-generated manipulations because they contain deepfakes produced with outdated or underdeveloped AI models.

- **Data Labeling Challenges:** To guarantee that no misclassifications take place, correctly classifying data as "real" or "fake" requires expert human validation.

- Some datasets only contain low-resolution deepfakes, which might cause models to perform poorly on higher-resolution, more realistic manipulations. This is known as the Low-Resolution vs. High-Resolution Bias.

2. Diversity and Representation Challenges

- **Demographic Bias:** A large number of deepfake datasets undergo poor performance on non-white faces and non-binary genders due to their training on Western-centric datasets that have an overrepresentation of white males.

- Deepfake datasets frequently lack diverse linguistic and cultural representations, which makes models less effective at identifying deepfakes in languages other than English.

3. Dataset Size and Variability

- **Need for Large-Scale Data:** Many datasets are very small (thousands of samples), yet deepfake detection algorithms need millions of examples to train efficiently.

Attack Method Variability: A dataset should include different deepfake generating techniques, such as:

- **Face-swapping** (such as FaceSwap and DeepFaceLab)
- **Lip-syncing** (Wav2Lip, for example)

The full-synthesis based on GAN theory (For instance, faces produced by StyleGAN)

Researchers must make sure datasets are diverse, accurately labeled, and large enough to capture real-world changes in order to construct robust detection systems.

5.2 Data Augmentation Techniques for Deepfake Detector Training

In order to increase dataset variety, enhance generalization, and avoid overfitting, data augmentation is crucial in deepfake detection. In order to handle undiscovered deepfake kinds, models must be trained on synthetically enlarged datasets due to the rapid advancement of deepfake technology.

1. Synthetic Data Generation

- **GAN-based Augmentation:** To generate fresh deepfake variations for training, researchers employ Generative Adversarial Networks (GANs).
- **Adversarial Deepfake Generation:** Models become more resilient to new attacks by continuously improving deepfake techniques and utilizing them in training.

2. Transformations of Images and Videos

Real and phony photos and videos can be altered in the following ways to increase robustness:

- Adjusting saturation, contrast, and brightness is

known as "color jittering."

- Rotation, scaling, and cropping are examples of spatial transformations that reflect real-world variances.

- A variety of video quality (low-resolution, high-resolution, compressed formats like MP4, AVI, etc.) are simulated by compression and noise injection.

3. Multimodal Data Augmentation

- **Audio Deepfake Variability:** To counteract voice-cloning deepfakes, add background noise, reverb, and pitch modifications.

- The process of creating synthetic text-based deepfake messages in order to train NLP-based detection algorithms is known as Text-Based Data Augmentation.

Deepfake detectors can generalize better across real-world conditions and become more reliable against undiscovered deepfake techniques by augmenting training datasets.

5.3 AI Detection Systems' Bias: Guaranteeing Equity Across Demographics

Algorithmic bias, the phenomenon where models perform noticeably better for some groups while failing for others, is one of the main problems in deepfake detection. Certain populations may be disproportionately affected by false positives or false negatives caused by bias in AI detection algorithms.

1. Common Biases in Deepfake Detection

- **Gender Bias:** Research has indicated that because males are overrepresented in training datasets, AI models are better at recognizing deepfakes on male faces than female faces.
- **Ethnic and Racial Bias:** The detection accuracy of darker-skinned individuals decreases if a dataset is skewed towards lighter-skinned individuals.
- **Age Bias:** Many deepfake datasets have insufficient representation of extremely young people and the elderly, which makes detection in these groups weaker.

In order to create fair and equitable deepfake detectors, researchers need to:

2. Addressing Bias in Deepfake Detection Models

- **Increase Training Datasets:** Make sure datasets are equal in terms of age, gender, and race.
- Employ fairness-aware ML techniques such as adversarial debiasing (see Use Bias-Reduction Algorithms).
- **Benchmark Across Demographics:** Evaluate models on various datasets to gauge amounts of bias and adjust as necessary.

3. Implications of AI Bias in the Real World

- **False Positives:** An AI model may mistakenly identify a genuine video of a member of an underrepresented group as a deepfake.
- **False Negatives:** The model may not identify deepfakes directed at minority groups, which could result in fraud and disinformation risks.

Deepfake detection systems must be trained and evaluated on varied, unbiased datasets that represent real-world populations in order to ensure fairness.

Ethical Considerations for Open vs. Proprietary Deepfake Detection Datasets

Two general criteria can be used to classify the availability of deepfake datasets:

1. Open Datasets (Accessible by the Public)

Examples include the Deepfake Detection Challenge Dataset, FaceForensics++, and Celeb-DF.

Benefits include:

- Encourages openness in AI research.
- Independent validation of detection methods is made possible.
- The research community can contribute in a variety of ways.
- One of the drawbacks is that open datasets can be used to train stronger deepfake generators, which makes detection more difficult.
- The presence of celebrity or public figure videos in certain databases raises ethical issues and raises privacy concerns.

2. Proprietary Datasets (Owned by Companies/Governments)

- Examples include Microsoft's Deepfake AI Challenge Data and Facebook's Deepfake Detection Dataset.

Benefits include:

- More thorough, current data.
- Better control over dataset security and quality.
- **The following are some drawbacks:** Restricted access for researchers.
- The possibility of bias if datasets are not independently verified.

Ethical Challenges in Dataset Usage

- **Informed Consent:** Do the people in the dataset know that their faces are being used to train artificial intelligence?
- Under the pretext of national security, should governments be able to impose restrictions on deepfake datasets?
- This is a dual-use concern. If datasets can be utilized to build better deepfake generators, should they be

made publicly available?

A balanced strategy is required: proprietary datasets should permit academic collaboration without compromising security, while open-source datasets should be thoroughly vetted.

Deepfake detection algorithms rely largely on the quality, diversity, and fairness of datasets to be effective. Taking on dataset difficulties entails:

The process of constructing diversified datasets that encompass all demographics.

- Enhancing the generalization of deepfake detectors through the use of data augmentation.
- To guarantee impartial and equitable deepfake detection, AI bias mitigation is necessary.
- Managing ethical issues between proprietary and open-source datasets.

Strong datasets are the cornerstone of reliable AI detection systems in the battle against deepfakes. Maintaining an advantage in the arms race between AI-generated forgeries and detection technologies requires creating objective, well-structured, and ethically sourced deepfake datasets.

CHAPTER 6

WATERMARKING AND FORENSIC ANALYSIS POWERED BY AI

The necessity for strong forensic analysis and watermarking techniques is more important than ever as deepfake technology develops. The detection of corrupted media is being aided by AI-powered forensic tools, while blockchain-based verification systems and watermarking are being developed to protect authenticity. This chapter examines these important technologies, their uses, and the difficulties in successfully putting them into practice.

6.1 Forensic AI: Following Digital Trails of Falsified Content

Deepfake detection is at the forefront of AI-driven forensic analysis, which uses a range of methods to find discrepancies in manipulated media. Inconsistencies in motion, illumination, biological signals, and pixel-level anomalies are all analyzed by these systems.

Key Forensic Techniques:

- **Pixel Anomaly Detection:** AI models examine the distributions of individual pixels to find anomalies brought forth by deepfake creation processes.

- **Motion Analysis:** AI-driven motion tracking is used to identify irregularities in lip synchronization, eye blinking, and facial emotions.

- **Biometric Verification:** To identify impersonation attempts, AI compares speech and facial biometrics to established profiles.

- **Compression Artifacts Analysis:** Analyzing video compression footprints aids in separating real content from artificial intelligence-generated media.

As an example: Researchers have created AI models that are able to identify deepfakes by using photoplethysmography signals, which are minute variations in facial blood flow, which deepfake algorithms frequently can't mimic.

Adversarial attacks that aim to trick detection models and the quick development of deepfake generation methods are two of the challenges that forensic AI must contend with, necessitating frequent upgrades to forensic tools.

6.2 Steganography and Watermarking: Integrating Authenticity Signals into Media

By adding visible or invisible markers to media files to certify authenticity, watermarking is becoming a proactive approach to thwart deepfakes. Watermarking enables confirmation before misinformation spreads, as opposed to reactive forensic detection.

Watermarking Technique Types:
1. **Visible Watermarking:** Text overlays or logos that are incorporated into media assets (for example, news organizations watermarking photos to stop illegal editing).
2. **Invisible (Steganographic) Watermarking:** Steganographic watermarking is the use of hidden signals that change pixel layouts or metadata and are only picked up by certain AI systems.
3. Fragile Watermarking: Watermarks that indicate tampering by distorting when altered.

4. **Sturdy Watermarking:** Watermarks that are not easily compressed, resized, or altered.

AI's Role in Watermarking: To identify and produce highly secure, imperceptible watermarks, even in the face of attacks that aim to erase or modify them, advanced AI models are being developed.

Difficulty: Deepfake producers are creating AI models that can remove watermarks, which is causing an arms race between adversarial attacks and watermarking solutions.

6.3 Blockchain for Digital Provenance Security: Media Verification

As a decentralized and tamper-proof approach to guaranteeing media authenticity, blockchain technology is being investigated. Any change to the media can be promptly verified by storing cryptographic hashes of the original media files on a blockchain ledger.

The Operation of Blockchain-Based Verification:

1. **Original Media Upload:** An picture, video, or audio

file is converted into a cryptographic hash and saved on a blockchain.

2. **Verification Process:** To look for inconsistencies, one might compare the hash of a suspicious file to the original recorded hash.

3. **Decentralized Security:** Media manipulation becomes very difficult due to the immutability of blockchain records.

Real-World Example: To confirm the validity of digital content, Adobe, Microsoft, and Twitter launched the Content validity Initiative (CAI), which integrates blockchain-like cryptographic signatures.

Difficulties: Blockchain transactions have a high processing cost.

Sensitive metadata stored on a public ledger raises privacy concerns.

Notwithstanding these problems, blockchain is a promising tool in the battle against deepfakes, particularly when paired with forensic tools that are based on artificial intelligence.

6.4 The Prospects of AI-Aided Media Authentication and Fact-Checking

AI-powered fact-checking and media authentication are increasingly crucial in newsrooms, social media platforms, and forensic investigations as deepfake technology advances.

New AI-Powered Fact-Checking Systems:

- **Automated Fake News Detection:** AI checks videos and articles for differences in factual correctness, style, and metadata.
- **Multimodal Analysis:** To identify false information produced by deepfakes, systems simultaneously examine text, images, and videos.
- **Crowdsourced AI Verification**: AI platforms enhance dependability by enabling journalists and experts to contribute to verification processes.

For instance: AI programs such as Microsoft's Video Authenticator employ deep learning to offer instantaneous confidence scores on the possibility of video manipulation.

The Road Ahead: Watermarking, blockchain verification, and AI-powered forensic analysis are expected to become more interconnected.

To stop false information from spreading, real-time deepfake detection systems will be integrated into key social media platforms. AI models will need to continuously adapt in order to combat emerging deepfake approaches.

AI-powered forensic analysis, watermarking, and blockchain verification are emerging as the cornerstones of deepfake detection as deepfake threats increase. Watermarking ensures content integrity, forensic AI aids in tracing manipulations, and blockchain offers an unchangeable record of authenticity. Defenders must, however, evolve rapidly as attackers improve their strategies, integrating these tactics to provide a comprehensive defense against synthetic media threats.

CHAPTER 7

GOVERNMENT AND INDUSTRY INITIATIVES TO FIGHT DEEPFAKES

Governments, tech businesses, and international organizations are taking action to reduce the hazards associated with deepfake technology as it develops. Although there are valid uses for deepfakes in education, entertainment, and accessibility, their abuse from political disinformation to fraud and defamation poses major risks to society.

Through policy, detection technology, legal frameworks, and digital literacy initiatives, this chapter explores how key technology corporations, governments, and global entities are addressing deepfakes.

7.1 The Role of Big Tech: How Microsoft, Google, and Meta Are Handling Deepfakes

Since their platforms are frequently the main means of disseminating manipulated content, leading tech corporations have a large stake in the fight against deepfakes. To stop the spread of dangerous deepfakes, these businesses are making significant investments in AI detection tools, content authenticity verification, and platform policies.

- Google's Efforts: In order to enhance detection models, researchers collaborated to create the Deepfake Detection Challenge (DFDC)
- Synthetic datasets have been made available by Google Research to aid in the training of deepfake detection algorithms.
- Google-owned YouTube has modified its policies to eliminate damaging AI-generated content, particularly that which is used to sway elections.

Meta's (Instagram and Facebook) Method

An AI-based deepfake detection system that was trained on a large amount of synthetic data.

- Put into effect regulations mandating that AI-generated content be clearly labeled.

- Collaborated with fact-checking groups to identify and limit the dissemination of false information produced by artificial intelligence.

- Investigating content provenance solutions to make sure submitted photos and videos have authenticated information.

The creation of Video Authenticator, an AI-powered tool that offers a real-time confidence score on whether a video has been modified, is one of Microsoft's initiatives.

- In order to prevent deepfakes during elections, we collaborated with the AI Foundation to develop Reality Defender 2020.

- Together with Adobe and Twitter, I helped develop standards for media authentication as part of the Content Authenticity Initiative (CAI).

Despite these efforts, deepfake producers are still creating new evasion techniques, necessitating ongoing innovation in detection models and policy enforcement.

7.2 The Government's Role: Policies and Laws to Combat Deepfakes

Deepfake technology is developing so quickly that governments throughout the world are finding it difficult to keep up. A comprehensive legal framework is still being developed in some nations, while some countries have introduced laws addressing malevolent deepfakes.

Primary Subjects of Law

1. Laws that specifically forbid the production and dissemination of deepfakes for the purposes of fraud, defamation, or election meddling are known as "criminalizing harmful deepfakes."

- Certain nations have specific laws against non-consensual pornography and sexual harassment based on deepfakes.

2. Election Integrity and Political Misinformation

A number of governments have enacted legislation mandating disclaimers on political advertisements and campaign materials produced by artificial intelligence.

- Intelligence agencies are required by the National Defense Authorization Act (NDAA) of the United States to report on foreign deepfake threats.
- To avoid spreading false information, deepfake producers in China are required to clearly mark AI-generated content.

3. Consumer Protection and Fraud Prevention

Rules mandating that social media platforms identify and eliminate deceptive deepfakes utilized in financial fraud and scams.

- Clauses that hold businesses responsible for not regulating synthetic media that damages people or companies.

Enforcing deepfake laws remains a challenge despite these attempts because of jurisdictional difficulties, creator anonymity, and rapid developments in AI-generated media.

7.3 Global Cooperation: Establishing International Guidelines for Deepfake Identification

In order to solve the issue on a global level, international cooperation is crucial because deepfake risks are not confined to national borders. Standardizing detection tools, exchanging threat intelligence, and building legal frameworks are the goals of several international efforts.

Present International Projects

1. The Global Partnership on AI (GPAI)

- A group of more than 25 countries collaborating to create moral standards and detection tools for reducing deepfakes.
- Concentrates on coordinating AI research to fight digital fraud and false information.

2. The EU's Digital Services Act (DSA)

- Demands that tech platforms" disclose more information on how they discover AI-generated content.
- For failure to control toxic synthetic media, sanctions are suggested.

3. Facebook, Amazon, Microsoft, and MIT are sponsors of the Deepfake Detection Challenge (DFDC), an initiative that attempts to improve AI detection systems by supplying various datasets for study.

In order to create international rules for responsible AI development, the UN has developed the AI Ethics Guidelines, which include safeguards against deepfake manipulation.

Difficulties in International Cooperation

- **Different legal frameworks:** What is prohibited in one nation could be considered free speech in another.
- The absence of standardized detection standards makes it challenging to deploy deepfake detection technologies on a broad scale because they differ across platforms and organizations.
- Geopolitical tensions: Because of national security concerns, several governments refuse to share AI research.

Despite these obstacles, building a worldwide deepfake detection ecosystem requires increasing international collaboration.

7.4 Digital Literacy and Public Awareness: Enabling Users to Recognize Deepfakes

While laws and technology are important in fighting deepfakes, a knowledgeable and tech-savvy populace is one of the most effective defenses. By enabling people to critically analyze online content and identifying deepfakes, users can reduce the spread of misinformation.

Important Techniques for Digital Literacy

1. Educational Campaigns

- **Deepfake awareness modules** are being incorporated into media literacy programs at colleges and institutions.
- Public awareness programs supported by the government and public service announcements (PSAs) assist citizens in identifying distorted media.

2. Online Tools for Deepfake Detection

- Users can analyze questionable photos and videos using browser extensions and AI-based verification tools.

- Publicly available deepfake detection tools are offered by companies such as Deepware Scanner and Sensity AI.

It is recommended that users confirm sources, seek for visual anomalies, and search for discrepancies in speech patterns and lip-syncing in videos in order to promote critical thinking.

In order to ensure ethical use in journalism and entertainment, platforms are pushing content creators to disclose the use of AI-generated material.

People become less susceptible to manipulation by increasing digital literacy efforts, which lessens the impact of deepfake misinformation on society.

A multi-layered approach is needed to combat deepfakes, combining AI-driven detection, stringent policies, international cooperation, and public education. Deepfake dangers are still evolving even while tech companies are developing improved detection tools, governments are implementing legal frameworks, and global organizations are moving toward standardization.

In the end, one of the best defenses is to empower the public with digital literacy. The risks associated with synthetic media can be reduced by society by encouraging critical thinking, awareness, and access to verification tools. To keep ahead of bad actors, governments, industry leaders, and researchers must continue to collaborate as AI-generated material gets more sophisticated.

CHAPTER 8

DEEPFAKE DETECTION: PRACTICAL USES AND CASE STUDIES

Deepfake technology's practical effects are becoming more noticeable in a variety of industries, including national security, entertainment, banking, and journalism, as it develops. Although there are valid applications for deepfake technology in accessibility and content production, its malicious applications pose serious concerns to truth, security, and public trust.

This chapter explores journalism, financial security, media ethics, and political risks through real-world case studies where deepfake detection has been crucial. These instances demonstrate the difficulties, repercussions, and continuous endeavors to combat deepfake manipulation.

8.1 Journalism's Deepfake Threats: Upholding the Truth in the Digital Era

The public now finds it more difficult to distinguish between real and fake content as a result of the rise of deepfakes, which have added a new dimension of misinformation to journalism. Deepfake technology can be used as a weapon to spread disinformation, discredit journalists, and manipulate public opinion, with dire consequences for democracy, the free press, and public confidence.

Case Study: Journalists Impersonated by Deepfakes

A video imitation of a reputable investigative journalist created by deepfake appeared online in 2021. Audiences became confused and mistrustful of the AI-generated clone since it was designed to make false statements about a political figure.

- Unaware of the video's existence, the journalist's reliability was called into question until forensic examination demonstrated that it was a fake.
- Deepfake detection techniques and fact-checkers were employed to analyze irregularities in speech modulation, facial movements, and unnatural lip-syncing.
- The deliberate use of the deepfake prior to a

significant election demonstrated how synthetic media can be used to sway political narratives.

Difficulties in Journalism Deepfake Detection

- **Quick Social Media Spread:** Once a deepfake is posted, it can go viral within hours, making damage control challenging.
- Many people without the tools and knowledge to distinguish between real sources and AI-generated information due to a lack of digital literacy.
- **Targeting of Journalists:** Deepfakes are being utilized more and more to injure news organizations, undermine press freedom, and discredit reporters.

In order to check videos for authenticity before to publication, newsrooms are including deepfake detection software into their Mitigation Strategies

- Adoption of AI-Powered Verification Tools.
- In order to flag and minimize the reach of deepfake content, fact-checkers are collaborating with social media platforms such as Facebook and Twitter.
- **Public Awareness Campaigns:** Programs like First Draft and MediaWise teach people how to identify

distorted media.

It takes consistent investment in detection tools, active fact-checking, and public education on misinformation tactics to maintain journalistic integrity in the age of AI-generated content.

8.2 AI-Generated Content in Cybersecurity and Finance: Techniques for Preventing Fraud

Deepfakes have created a new arena for cybersecurity risks and financial fraud, especially in the areas of corporate espionage, financial frauds, and identity theft. Attackers impersonate CEOs, government officials, and financial authorities using AI-generated voices, films, and photos, resulting in data breaches and financial losses.

The CEO Voice Scam Case Study

Cybercriminals used AI-generated voice cloning to pose as the CEO of an energy firm in the UK in 2019. The attackers directed an employee to transfer €220,000 ($243,000) to a bogus account by eerily mimicking the executive's voice.

The worker followed the directions because they thought the request was sincere.

- Forensic analysis did not prove the usage of an AI-generated deepfake voice until later.
- The crooks used publicly accessible speech recordings from conferences and media interviews to train the deepfake model.

Types of Deepfake Financial Fraud

- **Synthetic Identity Fraud:** Con artists create new identities for opening fraudulent accounts by combining actual and fake personal information.
- The use of AI-generated movies to disseminate misleading information about a company's leadership can lead to stock market manipulation.
- **Voice Cloning in Customer Support Fraud:** To get around security verification systems and get access to bank accounts, attackers imitate the voices of customers.

Detection and Prevention Strategies

- **Biometric Authentication Improvements:** To combat deepfake impersonation, financial institutions are turning to multi-factor authentication, behavioral analysis, and liveness detection.

- In order to identify deepfake scams, banks are utilizing AI-Driven Fraud Detection Systems to keep an eye on speech irregularities, voice patterns, and unusual audio modulations.

- **Regulatory Guidelines:** To ensure more stringent verification procedures, governments and financial watchdogs are creating anti-deepfake regulations for financial institutions.

The financial industry needs to adopt advanced authentication methods and make sure that employees are educated to spot deepfake scams in order to stay ahead of AI-driven threats.

8.3 Media and Entertainment: The Ethical and Legal Limits of Synthetic Content

Because deepfake technology allows for realistic CGI characters, digital de-aging, and posthumous performances, it has revolutionized entertainment. On the other hand, it raises ethical and legal concerns about permission, content ownership, and possible exploitation.

Case Study: Actors' Unauthorized Resurrection

- The late actor Peter Cushing was digitally recreated in Rogue One: A Star Wars Story in 2019 using deepfake technology.
- Despite being allowed by law, the reconstruction generated controversy over posthumous digital performances and consent.
- AI-generated appearances of deceased performers in performances and ads are examples of such cases.

Ethical and Legal Challenges in Entertainment

- **Consent and Copyright:** Should actors and public figures be compensated when their likeness is used in AI-generated content?
- **Misinformation Risks:** Can deepfake-generated content be used to rewrite history or manipulate real-world narratives?

Regulatory and Industry Reactions

- **Tougher Licencing Agreements:** To safeguard actor rights, studios are incorporating

AI-reproduction clauses in contracts.

- Platforms are advocating for the required labeling of entertainment content generated by artificial intelligence.

Legal Precedents in Copyright Laws: AI-generated likenesses are increasingly being recognized as intellectual property by courts.

Clear restrictions are necessary to ensure ethical AI use in media, even while deepfake technology offers exciting creative opportunities.

8.4 Deepfake Manipulation Case Studies: Political and National Security Risks

Deepfakes are a serious danger to national security and political stability, especially when it comes to election manipulation, propaganda, and diplomatic misinformation. In order to stop disinformation tactics, governments are making significant investments in deepfake detecting tools.

Events Case Study: Deepfake Misinformation

A deepfake video purporting to portray a political

candidate making provocative remarks went viral on social media in 2020.

- The film was eventually disproved, but not before it had swayed public opinion and gone viral.
- This demonstrated how synthetic media may influence elections and harm reputations.

Deepfake-Assisted Cyber Espionage: AI-generated impersonations have the potential to deceive government officials into disclosing confidential information.

- The use of deepfakes to fake statements from international leaders, igniting geopolitical tensions can cause diplomatic disruptions.
- **Recruitment for Extremist Organizations:** Deepfake videos have been used by terrorist organizations as a means of promotion and radicalization.

Government Strategies for Deepfake Defense

- **AI-Powered Deepfake Detection Labs:** To combat the dangers of synthetic media, intelligence organizations are creating in-house detection systems.

- **Legal Frameworks for Election Integrity:** Disclosure labels are now required in a number of nations for AI-generated political ads.

- **Cybersecurity Task Forces:** To detect and address deepfake threats, governments are educating national security teams.

In order to reduce the hazards posed by deepfakes, which have become a potent instrument for disinformation, international cooperation, AI-driven defensive systems, and public awareness campaigns are required.

In the fields of national security, entertainment, finance, and journalism, deepfake technology offers both opportunities and challenges. Although AI-generated material can improve storytelling, accessibility, and creativity, proactive protection tactics are necessary because of its misuse for deceit, fraud, and manipulation.

Through the development of detecting techniques, stringent restrictions, and the promotion of media literacy, society can capture the advantages of synthetic media while reducing its risks.

CHAPTER 9

THE PATH AHEAD FOR FUTURE-PROOFING DEEPFAKE DETECTION

The difficulty of identifying and reducing the negative consequences of deepfake technology is becoming more complicated as it develops. The development of advanced, flexible, and morally sound AI-driven solutions is essential to the future of deepfake detection. With an emphasis on quantum computing, self-supervised learning, human-AI collaboration, and ethical AI development, this chapter examines the most recent advancements in the field.

9.1 Quantum Computing's Effect on AI-Generated Media Recognition

A revolutionary shift in computer capacity, quantum computing has the potential to revolutionize deepfake detection using artificial intelligence. Utilizing quantum bits (qubits), which can exist in several states concurrently, quantum computing differs from traditional computing, which processes information in binary (0s and 1s). This feature revolutionizes deepfake detection by drastically increasing processing power.

Quantum computing's possible benefits for deepfake detection

The ability to recognize patterns more quickly and accurately Deepfake detection can be done more quickly and accurately thanks to quantum algorithms' ability to process enormous volumes of audio and video data in real-time.

- **Improved Feature Extraction:** Complex patterns in synthetic media can be analyzed by quantum machine learning, which can spot discrepancies that traditional AI algorithms might overlook.
- **Cracking Deepfake Network Encryption**: Many malevolent actors disseminate deepfakes over encrypted means. Law enforcement organizations may be able to disrupt these networks with the aid of quantum decryption skills.

But there are drawbacks to quantum computing as well:

Potential for Quantum-Powered Deepfakes: Quantum computing may help detect deepfakes, but it may also make it possible to create more complex and undetectable ones.

- **High Cost and Restricted Accessibility:** The technology of quantum computing is still in its infancy, with high operating costs and restricted availability.
- **Need for New Quantum-AI Hybrid Models**: In order to successfully include quantum computing capabilities, classical AI architectures must change.

In order to keep ahead of the competition as quantum computing advances, researchers must create deepfake detection systems that take advantage of quantum processing without creating new security flaws.

9.2 Self-Supervised Learning: AI Capable of Adjusting to New Deepfake Methods

Traditional supervised AI models eventually become ineffective due to the rapid evolution of deepfake technology. By allowing AI systems to learn from unlabeled data and continuously adapt to new deepfake techniques without requiring significant human intervention, self-supervised learning (SSL) offers a possible substitute.

The following are the main characteristics of self-supervised learning in deepfake detection:

Real-time adaptation is made possible by SSL models' ability to recognize deepfake patterns through automatic feature learning, which eliminates the need for pre-labeled datasets.

- **Generalization Across material Types:** These models do not need to be trained separately for each format in order to identify deepfakes in text-based, audio, and video-based synthetic material.
- **Decreased Reliance on Human-Labeled Data:** SSL is able to derive valuable representations from unlabeled data, whereas traditional supervised learning necessitates large labeled datasets.

SSL Use in Deepfake Identification:

The ability of AI models to continually watch live video streams and identify abnormalities suggestive of deepfake manipulation is known as "Anomaly Detection in Streaming Content."

- In order to stop the propagation of false information, SSL-powered AI is able to recognize deepfake patterns on a variety of social media sites.
- **Detection of New Deepfake Algorithms:** SSL allows AI models to keep up with new synthetic media approaches as generative adversarial networks (GANs) advance.

Researchers can develop more robust AI-driven solutions that can recognize complex manipulations by including self-supervised learning into deepfake detection systems.

9.3 Human-AI Cooperation: Improving Detection through Professional Supervision

AI is not perfect, even if it has shown great efficacy in identifying deepfakes. In order to improve detection accuracy, lower false positives, and handle ethical issues, human oversight is still essential. Deepfake detection's future depends on smooth human-AI cooperation.

The Function of Human Specialists in AI-Powered Deepfake Identification:

- **Finishing AI Models:** Digital forensics specialists can examine AI-generated deepfake reports and improve algorithms for increased accuracy.
- **Making Ethical Decisions:** Deepfake stuff isn't always harmful. AI won't mistakenly detect humor, artistic works, or innocuous changes thanks to human oversight.
- **Judicial and Investigative Applications:** Artificial intelligence (AI) techniques can help forensic analysts, but before legal action is taken, discoveries must be verified by human professionals.

Techniques for Successful Human-AI Cooperation:

- **Hybrid Detection Frameworks:** Increasing detection reliability can be achieved by combining expert assessment with AI-based analysis.

- **Explainable AI (XAI):** AI models must yield results that are comprehensible so that human analysts can comprehend and validate their conclusions.

- **Crowdsourced Verification Networks:** Deepfake Detection Challenges and similar platforms enable AI systems to gain knowledge from the combined wisdom of humans.

Deepfake detection systems can increase accuracy while lowering moral and legal hazards by encouraging cooperation between AI and human specialists.

9.4 Ethical AI Development: Media AI's Strike Between Innovation and Security

To avoid abuse, ethical considerations must direct the development of AI-generated media as it advances. Technologies for deepfake detection need to balance privacy, security, and creativity.

Moral Difficulties in Deepfake Identification:

- **Privacy Concerns:** Excessively aggressive deepfake detection may violate people's right to privacy, particularly if biometric information is examined without permission.

- **Censorship Risks:** Deepfake detection tools could be abused by governments and businesses to stifle dissent or impede artistic expression.

- **Bias in AI Models:** Deepfake detection AI may identify particular groups or categories of material disproportionately if trained on biased datasets.

Deepfake Detection Best Practices for Ethical AI:

Transparency in AI Decision-Making: Detection algorithms ought to be explicable so that interested parties may comprehend the decision-making process.

- **Regulatory Compliance:** Developers need to make sure deepfake detection tools comply with data protection regulations and international digital ethical standards.

- **Working with Ethical AI Organizations**: Collaborations with human rights and academic groups can help guarantee responsible AI development.

In order to ensure that AI continues to be a positive force, ethical constraints must be incorporated into deepfake detection in the future.

We are far from done fighting deepfakes. Deepfake detection must develop in tandem with the advancement of synthetic media technology. Unmatched processing capacity is provided by quantum computing, self-supervised learning permits ongoing adaptation, human-AI cooperation improves accuracy, and ethical AI development guarantees responsible innovation. Researchers and politicians may build a more robust defense against the escalating threat of deepfakes by using these future-proofing techniques.

CHAPTER 10

AN APPEAL FOR INTERVENTION IN THE BATTLE AGAINST DEEPFAKES

A new era of difficulties with media authenticity, cybersecurity, and public trust has been brought about by the rise of deepfakes. As AI-generated content gets more complex, protecting against its abuse calls for a multifaceted strategy that includes technology, policy, education, and international cooperation. In addition to outlining tactics for creating a robust defense system and stressing the importance of ongoing study and adaptation, this chapter summarizes the most important lessons learned from the fight against deepfakes and offers views into the future of synthetic media detection.

10.1 Important Conclusions and Knowledge Gained from the AI-Deepfake Conflict

Fighting deepfakes has been an ongoing learning process

that has provided important new information about the advantages and disadvantages of current detection techniques.

Important Takeaways from the Deepfake Conflict:

Deepfake technology is developing more quickly than anticipated. This is because AI-driven generative models, especially those built on generative adversarial networks (GANs), have advanced quickly, making deepfakes more realistic and challenging to identify.

- **The Target of Detection Is Moving:** Traditional detection approaches are rendered obsolete by the emergence of new deepfake techniques. To stay up, AI systems must be self-learning and adaptive.

- **Real-World Repercussions of Deepfakes:** The effects of synthetic media go beyond entertainment and endanger democracy, security, and trust through everything from financial fraud to political disinformation.

- **Education and Public Awareness Are Essential:** Deepfake detection relies heavily on technology, but digital literacy is just as crucial. To recognize and combat deepfake content, users require the necessary resources and expertise.

- The Deepfake Crisis Cannot Be Solved by a Single Solution: To effectively reduce the hazards, a mix of ethical AI development, government regulation, AI-powered detection, and industry cooperation is needed.

The knowledge gained from this continuous conflict emphasizes the necessity of a forceful and flexible strategy to combat the growing threat of deepfakes.

10.2 Developing a Robust AI-Powered Defense System to Counter Future Attacks

Beyond existing detection techniques, a strong deepfake defensive system must develop into a dynamic, AI-driven security architecture that can identify, stop, and mitigate synthetic media threats instantly.

Key Elements of a Robust Deepfake Defense Framework:

AI-Powered Detection Frameworks:

- Deep learning models that can recognize digital modifications in audio, video, and image formats.
- Algorithms for real-time detection of social media and live streaming content.
- Hybrid detection techniques that integrate behavioral, auditory, and visual analysis.

Blockchain for Media Authentication:

- Cryptographic verification methods to guarantee digital content authenticity.
- Immutable tracking and tagging of content to guard against manipulation.
- Decentralized verification systems that offer trust without being governed by a central authority.

Automated Response and Forensic Analysis:

- AI-powered forensic instruments capable of analyzing and reconstructing altered media.
- Cybersecurity and law enforcement organizations with deepfake forensic tools.
- Forensic analysis and legal procedures are integrated to counter false information.

Human Oversight and Expert Review:

- The use of hybrid human-AI models in which specialists verify deepfake alerts produced by AI.

- The establishment of impartial review panels to evaluate dubious content identified by AI.

- Collaborations across industries to create moral standards for deepfake verification.

Public Awareness and Reporting Mechanisms:

- Creation of publicly available, open-source deepfake detection tools.

- Digital literacy initiatives to educate deepfake detection methods in schools and workplaces.

- Social media rules should be strengthened to enable people to report suspicious deepfakes.

In order to stop the spread and effect of deepfakes, a well-designed AI-driven security system makes sure that the response is both preemptive and reactive.

10.3 The Value of Ongoing Study, Cooperation, and Adjustment

A single technological advancement won't be enough to win the war against deepfakes. It calls for sustained dedication to study, teamwork, and ongoing adaptation.

The Significance of Ongoing Research:

- Emerging Deepfake Techniques Demand New Detection Strategies: As AI models such as Google's Imagen, Meta's Make-A-Video, and OpenAI's DALL·E continue to improve their generative powers, new detection methods are required.
- Malicious actors are creating hostile deepfakes that can avoid detection by altering minute details in synthetic content. This indicates that adversarial AI is becoming more sophisticated.
- It's Possible That Quantum Computing Will Upend Conventional AI-Based Detection: Deepfake detection methods need to be ready for the opportunities and threats that come with the development of quantum AI.

The Value of Stakeholder Collaboration:

Industry Collaborations:

To speed up development, businesses like Google, Meta, and Microsoft need to exchange research results, best practices, and deepfake detection datasets.

- To guarantee ethical AI use while preventing abuse, AI developers must collaborate.

Coordination of Government and Policy:

- Nations must create uniform legal frameworks to combat crimes connected to deepfakes.
- Common protocols for dealing with cross-border deepfake threats should be established via international agreements.

Academic and Non-Profit Contributions:

- Research institutes and universities ought to keep looking into deepfake technology and its effects on society.
- Nonprofit groups can contribute to the promotion of digital ethics and public education.

Only a globally concerted effort can guarantee that deepfake detection continues to be successful against increasingly deceptive synthetic media as AI develops.

10.4 Looking Ahead: What Does Synthetic Media Detection Hold After 2025?

Technological innovation, legal development, and cultural adaptation will all play a part in deepfake detection in the future. Beyond 2025, a number of developments and trends are anticipated to influence the battle against the dangers posed by synthetic media.

Expected Developments in Deepfake Identification:

AI Models That Identify Deepfakes in Real Time
- State-of-the-art deep learning architectures that can identify deepfakes in real time.
- The incorporation of AI-powered detection technologies into news networks and social media platforms.

- Quantum machine learning models are used in Quantum-AI Hybrid Deepfake Detection Systems to detect even the smallest digital alterations.
- Watermarking technologies include quantum resistance to stop unwanted content changes.

Blockchain-powered authentication techniques to confirm the authenticity and origin of digital content are known as

Decentralized Verification Networks.

The public, fact-checkers, and independent journalists can all use open-source deepfake detection tools.

Changes in Law and Policy

More severe punishments for the deliberate production and dissemination of deepfakes.

- International agreement on digital content integrity and AI ethics.
- AI detection tools are required for social media and media sources.

AI education is included into school curricula to train the next generation how to handle deepfake threats, resulting in Enhanced Public Awareness and AI Literacy.

- Public awareness efforts to help internet users develop their deepfake detecting abilities.

- Programs for preparing reporters, law enforcement, and legislators to deal with cases involving deepfakes.

These developments will influence how people throughout the world react to synthetic media as deepfake technology develops further, guaranteeing that AI is used for truth rather than lies.

Although it is far from done, the fight against deepfakes is yet winnable. Society may create a strong defense against risks from synthetic media by utilizing AI-driven detection frameworks, encouraging ethical AI development, encouraging international cooperation, and placing a high priority on digital literacy. Adaptability is the key to future-proofing deepfake detection keeping up with bad actors through constant invention, research, and attention to detail. We must all do our part to combat deepfakes, and we can only protect the truth in the digital era by working together.

ABOUT THE AUTHOR

 Author and thought leader in the IT field Taylor Royce is well known. He has a two-decade career and is an expert at tech trend analysis and forecasting, which enables a wide audience to understand complicated concepts.

Royce's considerable involvement in the IT industry stemmed from his passion with technology, which he developed during his computer science studies. He has extensive knowledge of the industry because of his experience in both software development and strategic consulting.

Known for his research and lucidity, he has written multiple best-selling books and contributed to esteemed tech periodicals. Translations of Royce's books throughout the world demonstrate his impact.

Royce is a well-known authority on emerging technologies

and their effects on society, frequently requested as a speaker at international conferences and as a guest on tech podcasts. He promotes the development of ethical technology, emphasizing problems like data privacy and the digital divide.

In addition, with a focus on sustainable industry growth, Royce mentors upcoming tech experts and supports IT education projects. Taylor Royce is well known for his ability to combine analytical thinking with technical know-how. He sees a time when technology will ethically benefit humanity.

www.ingramcontent.com/pod-product-compliance
Lightning Source LLC
LaVergne TN
LVHW051704050326
832903LV00032B/3998

ISBN 9798309779666

90000

9 798309 779666